Star Signs

Brandon Robshaw and Rochelle Scholar

Published in association with The Basic Skills Agency

Hodder & Stoughton

A MEMBER

Basic Skills Collection

Acknowledgements
Cover: Jacey
Illustrations: Bridget Doherty
Photos: pp. 11, 14, 16, 20, 22, 24 © All Action.

Orders: please contact Bookpoint Ltd, 130 Milton Park, Abingdon, Oxon OX14 4SB.
Telephone: (44) 01235 827720, Fax: (44) 01235 400454. Lines are open from 9.00 – 6.00,
Monday to Saturday, with a 24 hour message answering service. Email address:
orders@bookpoint.co.uk

British Library Cataloguing in Publication Data
A catalogue record for this title is available from The British Library

ISBN 0 340 84868 5

First published 2002
Impression number   10 9 8 7 6 5 4 3 2 1
Year   2007 2006 2005 2004 2003 2002

Typeset by SX Composing DTP, Rayleigh, Essex.
Printed in Great Britain for Hodder & Stoughton Educational, a division of Hodder
Headline Plc, 338 Euston Road, London NW1 3BH by Bath Press Ltd.

Contents

1   What's Your Sign?

Almost everyone knows
what their star sign is.
Even people who don't believe in it.
It's one of those questions people ask at parties –
'What star sign are you?'
Nobody ever answers, 'I don't know.'

Many newspapers and magazines
have a horoscopes page.
Here you can read
what the stars have in store for you:
'You may come into money today.'
'There may be problems at work.'
'You may go on a journey soon.'
'Expect problems with your family today.'
'Today is a good day for starting
a new friendship.'
You will meet a tall dark stranger.'
And so on.

Even people who don't believe in it
read their horoscope.
It's just a bit of fun.
If we are promised good luck,
we can't help hoping it will come true.

If you think about it, though,
it's a very strange idea –
that the stars in the sky
can show what is going to happen to you.
Where does this idea come from?

2   Babylon

Reading the stars is sometimes called astrology.
It started two and a half thousand years ago
in Ancient Babylon –
now part of modern-day Iraq.

The people of Babylon noticed
that some stars seemed to move across the sky.
These stars are actually the planets of
Mercury, Venus, Mars, Jupiter and Saturn.

The people of Babylon believed that
the movements of the planets were
omens for the king.
His astrologers watched the planets to see
whether he would have good or bad luck.
But after a while, the people of Babylon
came to believe that the movements
affected everyone, not just the king.

3   The Zodiac

Around 330 BC, Babylon became
part of the Greek empire.
The people of Babylon taught astrology
to the Greeks.
The Greeks then perfected the system.

The basic idea of Greek astrology is this:
the Sun seems to move through groups of stars,
which are called constellations.
There are 12 constellations:
Aries (the ram), Taurus (the bull),
Gemini (the twins), Cancer (the crab),
Leo (the lion), Virgo (the virgin),
Libra (the scales), Scorpio (the scorpion),
Sagittarius (the archer), Capricorn (the goat),
Aquarius (the water carrier)
and Pisces (the fish).
These make up what is called the zodiac.

So if you were born at a time when
the sun was passing through the constellation
of Aries (21 March to 19 April),
your sign is Aries.

These are sun signs, which are used in
newspaper horoscopes.
But the Sun is not the only planet that
moves through the zodiac: the Moon, Mercury,
Mars, Jupiter and Saturn also do.
Proper astrologers look at the movements
of all these planets.

If an astrologer does
a personal horoscope for you,
he or she needs to know
the exact time and place that you were born.
Then they can work out exactly
where the Sun, the Moon, Mercury, Venus, Mars,
Jupiter and Saturn were when you were born.
All these planets are supposed
to have an effect on you.

4   A Science

A man called Claudius Ptolemy
made astrology into a science.
He charted the movements of all the planets.
He did this so exactly
that his calculations were used
for the next 1,500 years.

He also tried to explain
how and why the stars affect us.
The thought that the stars affect
the kind of person you are.
(For example, home-loving, kind,
bossy, and so on.)

This was different from what
the people of Babylon had thought.
They thought that the stars showed us
what was going to happen in our lives.
(For example, you are going to
come into a lot of money.)

Now astrologers believe what Ptolemy said:
that each sign has its own character.
Over hundreds of years,
the character of each sign has been built up
from studying the planets.

Proper astrologists say
it is not just the Sun that affects a
person's horoscope, but the other planets as well.
Here, we will just look at each sign in turn,
based on the position of the Sun at birth.

5   The Sun Signs

Ptolemy linked each constellation
with one of four elements:
fire, earth, air and water.
This was because he thought that there was
a link between all living things
and the four elements.
These elements are symbols
of the character of a sign.
There are three signs in each element group.

FIRE SIGN 1: ARIES

If you were born between 1 March
and 20 April you are Aries, the ram.
Aries is a fire sign, which symbolises
a physical and energetic character.

Aries people are full of life.
They are not shy people.
They are open to new ideas.
They love freedom.
Aries people also think about themselves a lot.

They can be selfish, restless and
have a quick temper.
Aries people do not like
taking advice from others.
They also do not like being wrong.

Famous people born under this sign
are Ewan McGregor and Russell Crowe.
Hitler was also an Aries.

FIRE SIGN 2: LEO

If you were born between 23 July and
22 August you are a Leo, the lion.

Leo people are the most
outgoing people in the zodiac.

You can rely on a Leo.
They have a warm heart and are giving.
Leos do not like having to watch their money.

They know what
they want from life and
they make sure they get it.
Leos can be bossy and look down on others.
Famous Leo people are Madonna
and Sandra Bullock.

FIRE SIGN 3: SAGITTARIUS

Sagittarius is the sign of the archer.
You are Sagittarius if you were born
between 23 November and 21 December.

Sagittarius people are full of life,
like Leo people.
They like to travel and to think
about many different things.

They are honest and truthful.
People born under this sign
like to fight for peoples' rights.

However, they can be restless, careless,
and say things without thinking.
They do not like
waiting for things to happen.
Famous people born under this sign
are Brad Pitt and Britney Spears.

Brad Pitt is Sagittarius, which means he is full of life.

WATER SIGNS 1: CANCER

Cancer, 22 June to 22 July,
is the sign of the crab.
This is a water sign.
Water signs are emotional.

Cancer people are home-loving.
People born under this sign
like to have a big family.
Their home is the place
that belongs to the family.

They are loving people
who like to protect others.
But, like a crab with its hard shell,
Cancer people may withdraw
into themselves.
They can be moody and clinging
and unable to let go.
Tom Hanks and Diana, Princess of Wales,
were born under this sign.

WATER SIGN 2: SCORPIO

If you are born between 24 October
and 22 November,
you are a Scorpio, the scorpion.
Scorpios are the most powerful
sign in the zodiac.
They are very forceful and exciting.
They like to do a job that has a purpose.
Many people are drawn towards Scorpios.
However, they can be very jealous people.
Sometimes, if their friends are
not useful to them, they drop them.
Scorpios also like having secrets.
Leonardo DiCaprio and Julia Roberts are Scorpios.

WATER SIGN 3: PISCES

The sign of the fish is called Pisces.
You are Pisces if you are born
between 20 February and 20 March.
Pisces people are easy-going.
They are more concerned about
other people's problems than their own.

They are emotional people
and can withdraw into their dream world.

Pisces people can be weak-willed
and easily led.
Like Scorpios, they like secrets.
Sharon Stone and Drew Barrymore
were born under this sign.

Drew Barrymore: easy-going Pisces.

EARTH SIGN 1: TAURUS

Taurus people were born between
21 April and 21 May.
This is the sign of the bull
and is an earth sign.
Earth signs are practical.

Taurus people are solid.
They can be gentle and loving.
They like comfort and pleasure
and time to think about things.
Taurus people are always
faithful to their friends.

They do not like to owe people money
and do not like change.
Taurus people are slow to anger.
However, if they are pushed too far
their temper can be violent.
George Clooney and Penelope Cruz
were born under this sign.
Shakespeare was also a Taurus.

Taurus people, like George Clooney, can be gentle
and loving.

EARTH SIGN 2: VIRGO

If you were born
between 23 August and 23 September
you are Virgo, the sign of the virgin.
People born under this sign
do not seem to show their feelings.
They make few friends.
They may seem shy.
Yet they are still waters
that run deep.
Deep down, they are caring people.

Virgos like to work hard
and they like order.
Virgos also like things to stay the same.
They do not like change.

Sean Connery and Tim Henman
are both Virgos.
So is the Queen.

EARTH SIGN 3: CAPRICORN

Capricorn is the sign of the goat.
If you are born between 22 December
and 20 January you are a Capricorn.
Capricorns are serious people.
They have a strong will and are calm.
Capricorns are hard-working
and do not like taking risks.

They put their family and their work
before their own needs.
They set high standards for themselves.
However, Capricorns do not like
spending their money.
Sometimes they can be too
set in their ways.

Nicolas Cage and Tiger Woods
are both Capricorns.
Elvis Presley was also born under this sign.

AIR SIGN 1: GEMINI

Gemini is the sign of the twins.
Gemini people are born between
22 May and 21 June.
Gemini people like to do
new things all the time.
They are lively people.
Life is a game to them.
Geminis are kind and polite.
They like to help the poor.

Geminis do tend to worry a lot.
They may also be a bit nervous.
Although they are able to adapt,
they can become unsure of themselves.
Geminis like to get what they want.
Nicole Kidman and Johnny Depp
were born under this sign.
So was Marilyn Monroe.

Johnny Depp is a Gemini, the sign of the twins.

AIR SIGN 2: LIBRA

People born between 24 September
and 23 October are Libra, the scales.
All the other signs are shown as
humans or animals.

Some astrologers think this is the best sign to be.
People born under this sign
are often good looking.
They have good taste and charm.
They are gentle, kind and easy-going.
They are the sort of people
who make you feel better
for having been with them.

However, if they make up
their mind about something,
they think other people
should think the same as them.
Librans can also shock
with a sudden show of anger.

Kate Winslet and Gwyneth Paltrow
were both born under this sign.

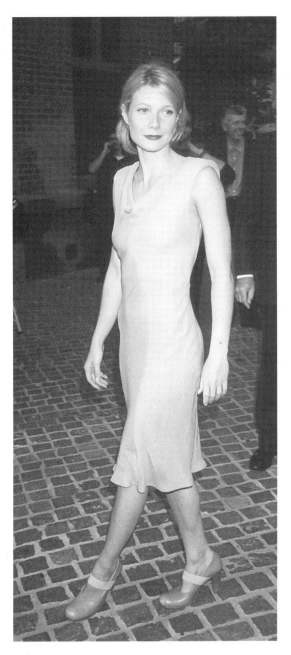

Is Gwyneth Paltrow a typical Libran?

AIR SIGN 3: AQUARIUS

Aquarius is the sign of the water carrier.
If you are Aquarius, your birthday
is between 21 January and 19 February.
Aquarius people may be shy and gentle.
They may also be lively show-offs.
Aquarius people have a strong will.

They like to seek the truth.
The people born under this sign
are friendly, honest and are clear thinkers.

Aquarians are good at seeing
another person's point of view.
They like to fight for causes.
Sometimes they like to be on their own.

Aquarians do not make friends easily.
They can be rude and cunning.
Like Librans, they can have a
sudden show of temper.
Jennifer Aniston and Michael Jordan
were both born under this sign.

Aquarius: Jennifer Aniston.

6 Copernicus

Astrology was a serious science
for 1,500 years.
All over Europe people believed in it.
Then it spread to India and the Arab world.

But in 1543 something happened.
A Polish scientist published a new theory.
His name was Copernicus.
He said that the Earth went round the Sun.
Until then, everyone had thought
that the Sun went round the Earth.

This changed everything.
The Earth was no longer
the centre of the universe.

The Sun didn't really travel
round the earth,
or pass through the constellations
of the zodiac.
It just looked as if it did.

Of course, it was still possible to believe
that the stars affected people.
But it seemed much less likely.

From this point on,
there was a split
between astrology and astronomy.

Astrology meant trying to read the stars.
Astronomy meant simply watching
and studying their movements.

Astrology wasn't seen
as a science any more.
Astronomy was the new science.

7 Astrology Today

Astrology is still popular today.
But it is a form of entertainment,
not a science.

We now know much more about the universe
than the ancient astrologers did.
Astronomers have discovered new planets
that the ancient astrologers didn't know about,
such as Pluto.
The stars are much further away
than was once thought.
The light from the nearest one
takes four years to reach us.

It's hard to believe that something so far away
could affect people's characters.
The biggest problem for astrology is that
there is simply no proof that it is true.

Still, astrology may not be a science today
but it once was.
It's thanks to astrologers that we
learned so much about the stars.
It's thanks to astrologers
that we have astronomy.
We should respect astrology
as a system that played a big part
in European thought for 2,000 years.

Even if it's not true,
it's still fascinating.
Most of us will still read
our horoscopes in the newspapers.

And when we read that the Sun
in our sign next month means
we will come into a lot of money,
we might just believe it –
or at least we might want to!